ENGLISH TOWN

FOR EVERYONE

BOOK 2

Contents

Characters

Leo

Corinne

Jean

Rachel's mom

Rachel

Mathis

Hello Song

Hello, everyone.
Hello, teacher!
Hello, friends!

Let's have fun together.
We'll have a good time.

Are you ready to start?
We're ready!

Here we go!

Goodbye Song

Did you have fun?

It's time to say goodbye.
See you next time!
See you next time!

Did you enjoy the class?
Yes! We had a fun time!
Yes! We had a fun time!

See you later! See you later!
Goodbye. Goodbye.

Bye! Bye!

The Way to the Eiffel Tower

Let's Talk

A. Look, listen, and repeat.

I'm not sure.

Are we lost?

Excuse me. How can I get to the Eiffel Tower?

Go straight and turn right at the bookstore.

BOOKSTORE

ACT IT OUT

Are we lost?

B. Listen and practice.

Go straight and turn right at the bookstore.

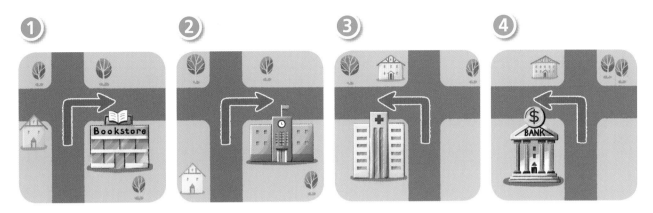

1 turn right at the bookstore

2 turn right at the school

3 turn left at the hospital

4 turn left at the bank

C. Listen, point, and say.

A: How can I get to the Eiffel Tower?
B: Go straight and turn right at the bookstore.

Let's Learn

A. Listen and chant.

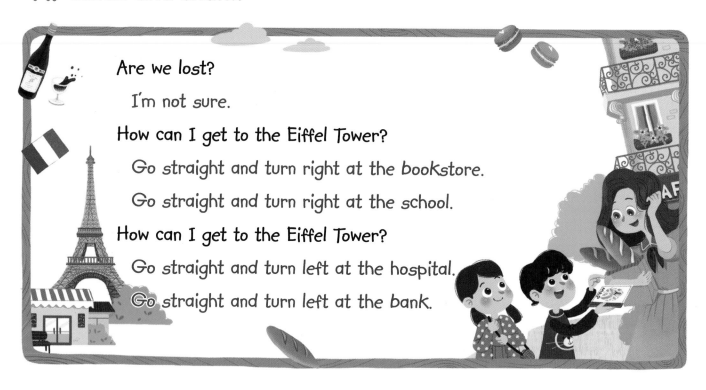

Are we lost?

I'm not sure.

How can I get to the Eiffel Tower?

Go straight and turn right at the *bookstore.*

Go straight and turn right at the *school.*

How can I get to the Eiffel Tower?

Go straight and turn left at the *hospital.*

Go straight and turn left at the *bank.*

B. Look, read, and match.

A: How can I get to the Eiffel Tower?

B: Go straight and _____.

❶

❷

❸

ⓐ turn left at the hospital

ⓑ turn right at the bookstore

ⓒ turn left at the bank

C. Fill in the blanks.
Then, ask and answer.

> A: How can I get to the Eiffel Tower?
> B: Go straight and turn right at the bookstore.

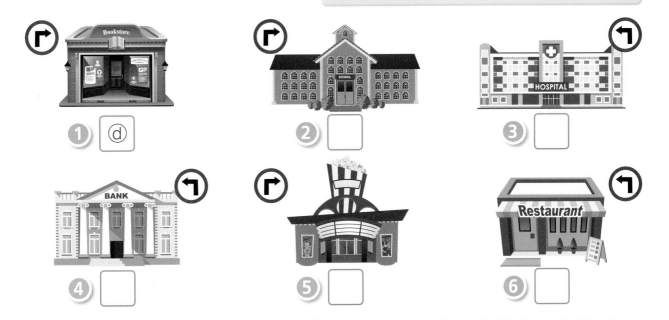

① d
② ▢
③ ▢
④ ▢
⑤ ▢
⑥ ▢

ⓐ turn left at the bank
ⓑ turn right at the movie theater
ⓒ turn left at the restaurant
ⓓ turn right at the bookstore
ⓔ turn right at the school
ⓕ turn left at the hospital

D. Work with your friends.

- Talk with your partner about how to get to the places on the map.

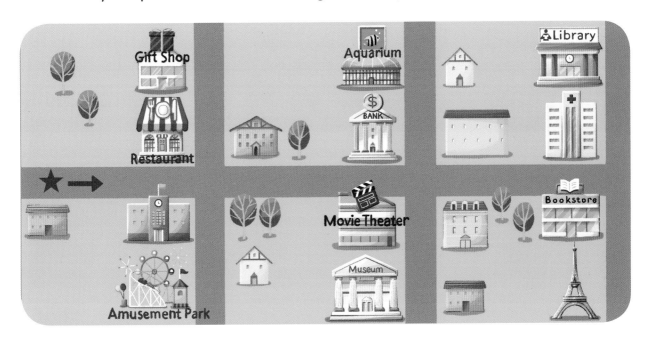

2 Where We Are From

Let's Talk

A. Look, listen, and repeat.

B. Listen and practice.

I'm from Canada.

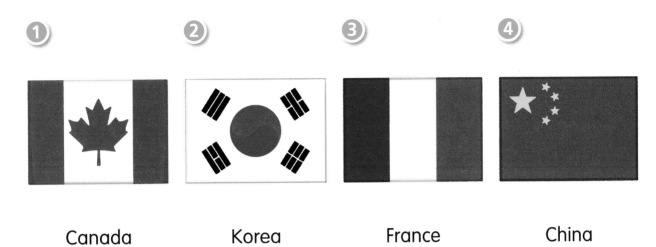

① Canada ② Korea ③ France ④ China

A: Where are you from?
B: I'm from Canada.

C. Listen, point, and say.

A. Listen and chant.

Would you like to join me?

Sure. Sure.

Where, where, where are you from?

I'm from Korea.

I'm from Canada.

Where, where, where are you from?

I'm from France.

I'm from China.

B. Listen and number the pictures.

C. Match, ask, and answer.

A: Where are you from?
B: I'm from Canada.

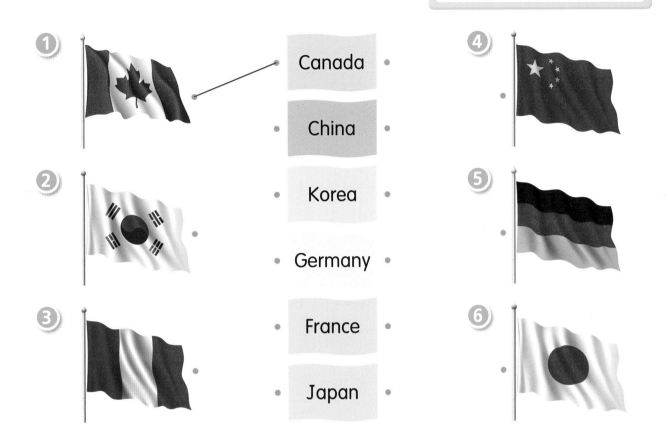

① Canada

② China

Korea

Germany

③ France

Japan

④

⑤

⑥

D. Work with your friends.

- Talk with your friends about where you are from.

Where are you from?

I'm from Korea.

A Trip to London

A. Listen and repeat the story.

B. Listen and number the pictures.

Baba   Inky

C. Read and circle.

1 How can Baba and Inky get to Big Ben?
- They can get there if they go straight and turn right at (the bank / the school / the restaurant).

2 Where is Baba from?
- He's from (Canada / Korea / France).

D. Choose a national flag and do a role-play.

A. Listen and sing.

How Can I Get to Big Ben?

Are we lost?

I'm not sure.

Excuse me. How can I get to Big Ben?

Go straight and turn right at the bank.

Would you like to join me?

Sure.

Where are you from?

I'm from China.

B. Play a board game.

♥ How can I get to the Eiffel Tower?
- Go straight and turn _____ at the _____.

★ Where are you from?
- I'm from _____.

16

e-learning

An Icon of London: Double-Decker Red Buses

London's double-decker red buses are world famous. They have two stories. If you want to take the bus, you can find a bus stop along all of the roads in London.

If you are seated in the front row on the top deck of the bus, you can enjoy sightseeing in London much better. The bus goes past Westminster Abbey, Big Ben, and Tower Bridge. Wouldn't it be fun to ride on a double-decker red bus?

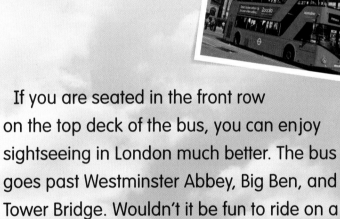

Check It Out!

1. What is one of the world-famous icons of London?
2. Which seat on the red bus is the best for sightseeing in London?

Travel Plans

A. Look, listen, and repeat.

18

B. Listen and practice.

We'll stay until next week.

① next week   ② tomorrow   ③ this weekend   ④ next Friday

A: How long will you stay?
B: We'll stay until next week.

C. Listen, point, and say.

14 : Today

A. Listen and chant.

Are you traveling? Are you traveling?

Yes, we are. Yes, we are.

How long will you stay?

We'll stay until next week.

Are you traveling? Are you traveling?

Yes, we are. Yes, we are.

How long will you stay?

We'll stay until this weekend.

B. Listen and number.

e-learning

C. Match, ask, and answer.

A: How long will you stay?
B: We'll stay until next week.

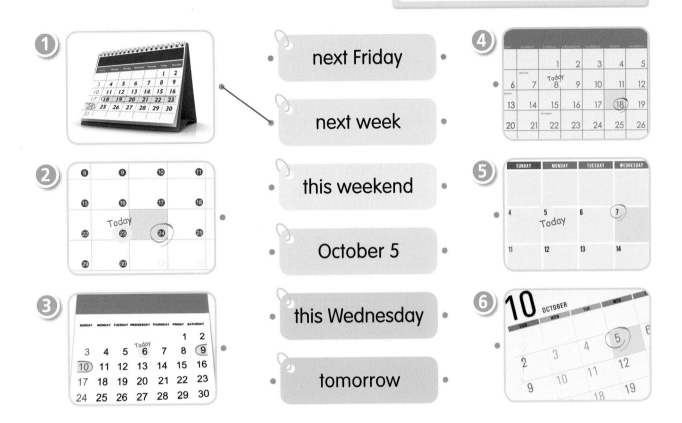

next Friday

next week

this weekend

October 5

this Wednesday

tomorrow

D. Work with your friends.

- Make your travel plans and ask your friends about their plans.

Travel Plans

• Where _____

• When _____

• How long _____

• What you want to do

_____

Speaking a Foreign Language

Lesson 5

Let's Talk

A. Look, listen, and repeat.

Act It Out

Thank you.

B. Listen and practice.

| French | Korean | German | English |

C. Listen, point, and say.

A. Listen and chant.

Can you speak English?

Yes, I can. Yes, I can.

You speak English very well.

Oh, thank you. Oh, thank you.

Can you speak French?

No, I can't. No, I can't.

Can you speak Korean?

Yes, I can. Yes, I can.

Passport Control

B. Break the code and match.

★a ▽c ●e ◇g ■h ◎i ▲l ◁m
♥n ◆o ♠r ◐s ♣E ◉K ◆F ▣G

1 Can you speak
◉◆♠♠●★♥?

2 Can you speak
♣♥◇▲◎◐■?

3 Can you speak
▣●♠◁★♥?

4 Can you speak
◆♠●♥▽■?

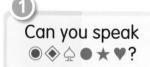 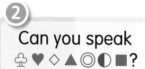 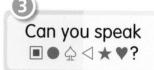 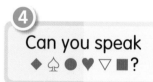

a Bonjour.

b Hi.

c 안녕.

d Guten Tag.

e-learning

C. Ask and answer.
Then, complete the faces.

A: Can you speak French?
B: No, I can't. ☹
   [Yes, I can. ☺]

① Bonjour.

French ☹

② 안녕.

Korean ☺

③ Guten Tag.

German ☺

④ Hi.

English ☺

⑤ 你好。

Chinese ☺

⑥ こんにちは。

Japanese ☺

D. Work with your friends.

- Ask your friend which languages he / she can speak.

Can you speak English?

Yes, I can.

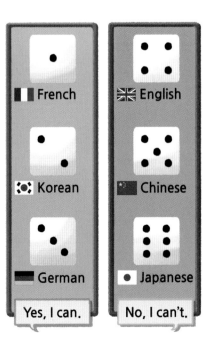

·	French	:: English
:·	Korean	::: Chinese
::·	German	:::: Japanese
Yes, I can.		No, I can't.

A Trip to Beijing

A. Listen and repeat the story.

B. Listen and number the pictures.

C. Read and match.

1 How long will Baba and Inky stay? •

• ⓐ They'll stay until next Tuesday.
• ⓑ They'll stay until this weekend.

2 Can Inky speak Chinese? •

• ⓐ Yes, she can.
• ⓑ No, she can't.

D. Choose a language and do a role-play.

Let's Play

A. Listen and sing.

You Speak English Very Well

Are you traveling?
   Yes, we are. Yes, we are.
How long will you stay?
   We'll stay until next week.
You speak English very well.
   Oh, thank you. Oh, thank you.
Can you speak Korean?
   No, I can't. No, I can't.

B. Play a board game.

■ : Today

★ Can you speak _____?
   - No, I can't. [Yes, I can.]

♥ How long will you stay?
   - We'll stay until _____.

The Forbidden City

The Forbidden City is the best-preserved and largest palace complex in the world. It is located in the heart of Beijing, China.

The Forbidden City is very large. It includes 90 palaces, 980 total buildings, and at least 8,700 rooms. Can you imagine how big it is?

The roofs of the buildings were made with yellow tiles. The reason is that yellow symbolized the emperor.

Check It Out!

1. Where is the Forbidden City located?
2. Why were the roofs of the buildings made with yellow tiles?

Lesson 7 Famous Places

Let's Talk

A. Look, listen, and repeat.

BOULANGERIE PATISSERIE

They look delicious, don't they?

Yes, they do.

Is this a famous bakery?

Yes, it is.

ACT IT OUT

They look delicious, don't they?

B. Listen and practice.

Is this a famous bakery?

bakery   library   hotel   park

C. Listen, point, and say.

A: Is this a famous bakery?
B: Yes, it is.

A. Listen and chant.

They look delicious, don't they?

Yes, they do. Yes, they do.

Is this a famous **bakery**?

Is this a famous **library**?

Yes, it is. Yes, it is.

Is this a famous **hotel**?

Is this a famous **park**?

Yes, it is. Yes, it is.

B. Look, read, and circle.

1

A: Is this a famous (library, bakery)?
B: Yes, it is.

2

A: Is this a famous (park, library)?
B: Yes, it is.

3

A: Is this a famous (hotel, bakery)?
B: Yes, it is.

C. Check, ask, and answer.

> A: Is this a famous bakery?
> B: Yes, it is.

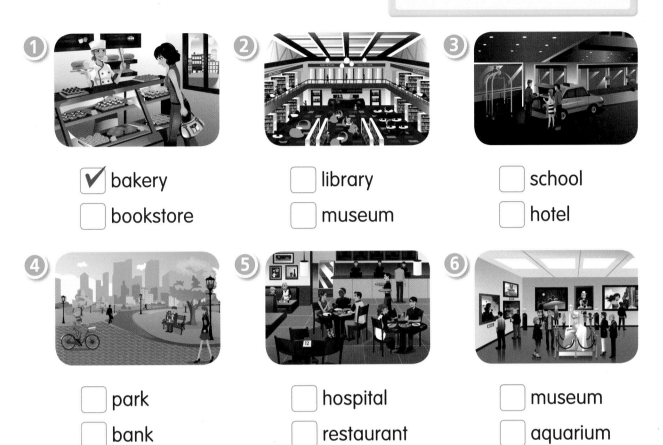

① ☑ bakery
☐ bookstore

② ☐ library
☐ museum

③ ☐ school
☐ hotel

④ ☐ park
☐ bank

⑤ ☐ hospital
☐ restaurant

⑥ ☐ museum
☐ aquarium

D. Work with your friends.

- Draw a famous place in your city and talk with your partner about it.

Is this a famous bakery?

Yes, it is.

The Juice You Want

A. Look, listen, and repeat.

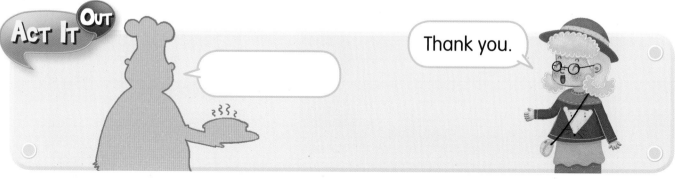

B. Listen and practice.

I want kiwi juice.

① kiwi juice   ② strawberry juice   ③ grape juice   ④ melon juice

C. Listen, point, and say.

A: What kind of juice do you want?
B: I want kiwi juice.

A. Listen and chant.

CAFE

What kind of juice do you want?

I want grape juice.

I want melon juice.

What kind of juice do you want?

I want strawberry juice.

I want kiwi juice.

Try this pie. Try this pie.

Thank you. Thank you.

B. Listen and match.

1 •

2 •

3 •

• a KIWI

• b GRAPE Juice

• c Strawberry

C. Go down the ladder.
Then, ask and answer.

A: What kind of juice do you want?
B: I want kiwi juice.

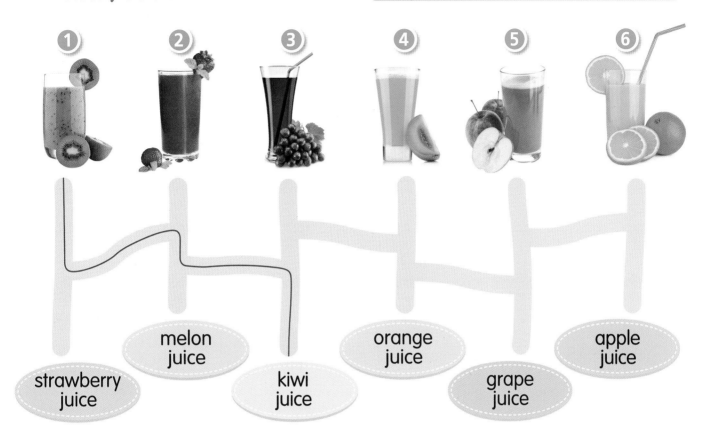

strawberry juice

melon juice

kiwi juice

orange juice

grape juice

apple juice

D. Work with your friends.

- Do a survey.

Name	Juice
Hana	strawberry juice

What kind of juice do you want?

I want strawberry juice.

A Trip to Prague

Is this a famous bakery?

Yes, it is.

They look delicious, don't they?

Yes, they do.

A. Listen and repeat the story.

B. Listen and number the pictures.

○   ○   ○   ○

C. Read and check True or False.

1. The bakery is famous. True ☐ False ☐

2. Baba doesn't have any bread. True ☐ False ☐

3. Inky wants orange juice. True ☐ False ☐

D. Choose a juice and do a role-play.

 ☐  ☐  ☐

A. Listen and sing.

Is This a Famous Bakery?

Is this a famous bakery?

Yes, it is. Yes, it is.

They look delicious, don't they?

Yes, they do. Yes, they do.

Pie, pie. Try this pie.

Thank you.

What kind of juice do you want?

I want kiwi juice.

B. Play a board game.

♥ What kind of juice do you want?
- I want _____.

★ Is this a famous _____?
- Yes, it is.

Czech Marionettes

What is a marionette? It's a string puppet. You can move its parts by using strings.

Czech marionettes are famous all around the world. They are made from wood or plaster. All kinds of characters from devils and wizards to kings and princesses are represented.

If you are traveling in the Czech Republic, how about seeing a marionette performance? It will be a great memory for you.

Check It Out!

1. How are marionettes worked?
2. What are marionettes made from?

 **Lesson 10** Assessment Test 1

A. Listen and check.

①

a. ☐   b. ☐

②

a. ☐   b. ☐

③

a. ☐   b. ☐

④

a. ☐   b. ☐

⑤

a. ☐   b. ☐

⑥

a. ☐   b. ☐

B. Listen and answer the questions.

① What language can Sue speak?

a. French   b. Korean   c. English

② What kind of juice does Evan want?

a. grape juice   b. kiwi juice   c. strawberry juice

A. Look, listen, and reply.

B. Number the sentences in order and talk with your partner.

◯ Go straight and turn left at the hospital.

◯ Would you like to join me?

① Excuse me. How can I get to the Eiffel Tower?

◯ Sure.

A. Read and match.

1. Is this a famous park? •   • a. I'm from Korea.

2. How can I get to the   •   • b. Yes, it is.
   Eiffel Tower?

3. Can you speak French?   •   • c. We'll stay until next week.

4. What kind of juice do you •   • d. Yes, I can.
   want?

5. Where are you from?   •   • e. I want melon juice.

6. How long will you stay?   •   • f. Go straight and turn right at
                                            the school.

B. Read and check True or False.

Excuse me. How can I get to the Eiffel Tower?

Go straight and turn right at the bookstore.

Thank you.

My pleasure. Are you traveling?

Yes, I am.

Where are you from?

I'm from Canada.

Daniel   Mary

1. Mary doesn't know how she can get to the Eiffel Tower. .... True ☐   False ☐

2. Daniel is traveling in France. .... True ☐   False ☐

3. Daniel is from Canada. .... True ☐   False ☐

e-learning

Korean   library   China   next Friday
strawberry juice   turn left at the bank

A. Write the words and phrases.

 ①

 ②

 ③

 ④

_____

_____

⑤

⑥

Can you speak

_____ ?

Is this a famous

_____ ?

B. Write the answers.

① A: How can I get to the Eiffel Tower?

B: _____

(turn / and / right / at / straight / the / go / bookstore / .)

② A: Where are you from?

B: _____

(from / I'm / Canada / .)

③ A: What kind of juice do you want?

B: _____

(want / I / kiwi juice / .)

The Four Seasons

Let's Talk

A. Look, listen, and repeat.

ACT IT OUT

B. Listen and practice.

I like spring.

① spring ② summer ③ fall ④ winter

A: What season do you like the most?
B: I like spring.

C. Listen, point, and say.

Let's Learn

A. Listen and chant.

What lovely weather!
What lovely weather!
   Yes, it is. Yes, it is.

What season do you like the most?
   I like winter. Winter.
What season do you like the most?
   I like summer. Summer.

B. Look, read, and match.

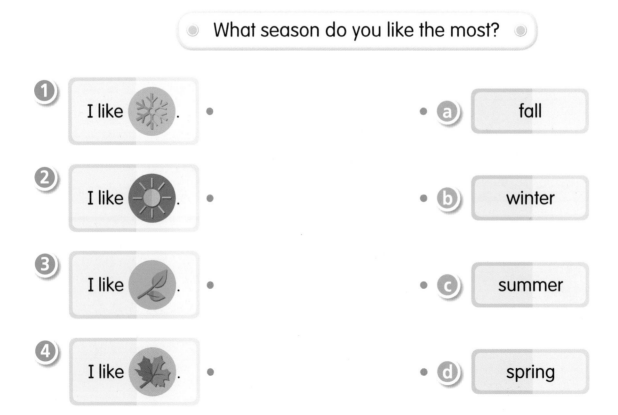

What season do you like the most?

1. I like ❄️ . •

a. fall

2. I like ☀️ . •

b. winter

3. I like 🍃 . •

c. summer

4. I like 🍁 . •

d. spring

C. Go down the ladder. Then, ask and answer.

A: What season do you like the most?
B: I like spring.

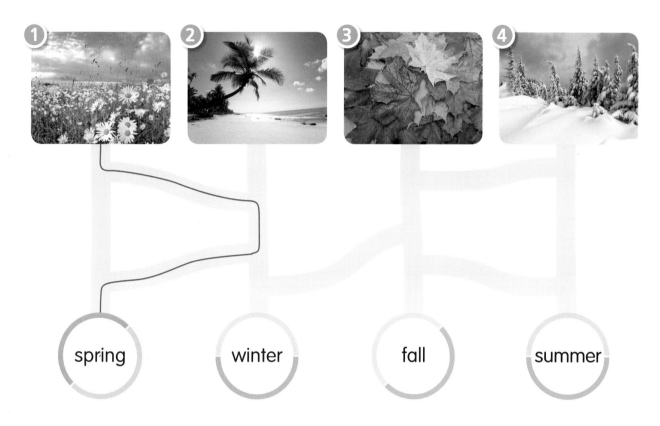

① ② ③ ④

spring   winter   fall   summer

D. Work with your friends.

- Draw the season that you like the most and talk about it with your friends.

What season do you like the most?

I like spring.

Time to Say Goodbye

A. Look, listen, and repeat.

It was nice meeting you.

You, too. Good luck.

Do you mind if I take a picture with you?

Not at all.

Rachel & Mathis

ACT IT OUT

You, too. Good luck.

50

B. Listen and practice.

Do you mind if I take a picture with you?

① take a picture with you

② give you a hug

③ send you an email

④ call you

C. Listen, point, and say.

A: Do you mind if I take a picture with you?
B: Not at all.

A. Listen and chant.

It was nice meeting you.

You, too. Good luck.

Do you mind if I take a picture with you?

Not at all. Not at all.

Do you mind if I send you an email?

Not at all. Not at all.

B. Listen and number the pictures.

C. Ask and answer.

A: Do you mind if I take a picture with you?
B: Not at all.

1
take a picture with you

2
give you a hug

3
send you an email

4
call you

5
write a letter

6
send you a text message

D. Work with your friends.

- Ask your friends what you want to do.

Do you mind if I _____?

A Trip to Brazil

A. Listen and repeat the story.

B. Listen and number the pictures.

C. Read and check.

1. What season does Baba like the most?

    a) spring   b) summer   c) fall

2. What does Inky ask Tucan ?

    a)   b)   c)

D. Choose the season you like and do a role-play.

A. Listen and sing.

Do You Mind If I Take a Picture with You?

What lovely weather!
  Yes, it is. Yes, it is.

What season do you like the most?
  I like fall. I like fall.

Do you mind if I take a picture with you?
  Not at all. Not at all.

  It was nice meeting you.
    You, too. Good luck.

B. Play bingo.

★ Do you mind if I _____ ?
  - Not at all.

♥ What season do you like the most?
  - I like _____ .

The Rio Carnival in Brazil

Brazil is famous for its carnivals. Rio de Janeiro is a city known for the Rio Carnival. The carnival is held in spring to celebrate the arrival of spring.

The highlight of the carnival is the Samba Parade. During the parade, the streets are filled with music and dancing. If you are there, you cannot help dancing.

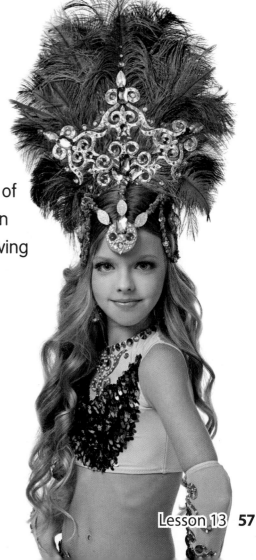

The Rio Carnival is one of the biggest attractions on the Earth. How about having fun in Rio de Janeiro?

Check It Out!

1. Why is the Rio Carnival held in spring?
2. What is the highlight of the Rio Carnival?

14 The Price of the Dress

Let's Talk

A. Look, listen, and repeat.

Look. It's a flea market.

Let's go and see.

How much is this dress?

It's 20 euros.

ACT IT OUT

Look. It's a flea market.

B. Listen and practice.

How much is this dress?

① dress ② T-shirt ③ sweater ④ coat

C. Listen, point, and say.

A: How much is this dress?
B: It's 20 euros.

A. Listen and chant.

Look. Look. It's a flea market.

Let's go and see.

How much is this dress?

20. 20. It's 20 euros.

How much is this T-shirt?

5. 5. It's 5 euros.

How much is this sweater?

10. 10. It's 10 euros.

B. Listen and choose.

① €10   ⓐ   ⓑ

② €5   ⓐ   ⓑ

③ €20   ⓐ   ⓑ

④ €10   ⓐ   ⓑ

C. Fill in the blanks.
Then, ask and answer.

A: How much is this dress?
B: It's 15 euros.

1 €15 dress

2 € T-shirt

3 € sweater

4 € coat

5 € jacket

6 € skirt

D. Work with your friends.
- Hold a charity bazaar.

₩ 1,000

• What I bought

1 _____

2 _____

3 _____

• What I sold

1 _____

2 _____

3 _____

15 Having Some Hot Dogs

Let's Talk

A. Look, listen, and repeat.

So am I.

I'm getting hungry.

How about having some hot dogs?

Sounds like a good idea.

ACT IT OUT

I'm getting hungry.

B. Listen and practice.

How about having some hot dogs?

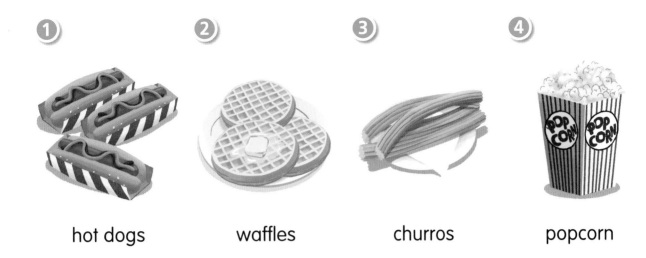

① hot dogs ② waffles ③ churros ④ popcorn

A: How about having some hot dogs?
B: Sounds like a good idea.

C. Listen, point, and say.

A. Listen and chant.

I'm getting hungry.

So am I. So am I.

How about having some hot dogs?

How about having some waffles?

Sounds like a good idea.

How about having some churros?

How about having some popcorn?

Sounds like a good idea.

B. Break the code and read the sentences.

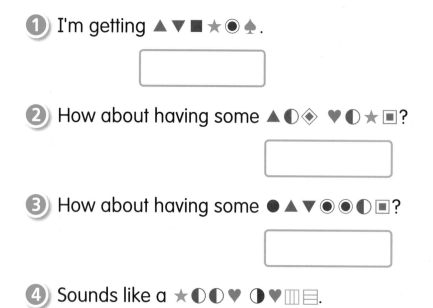

1 I'm getting ▲▼■★◉♠.

2 How about having some ▲◑◈ ♥◑★▣?

3 How about having some ●▲▼◉◉◑▣?

4 Sounds like a ★◑◑♥ ◑♥▥◨.

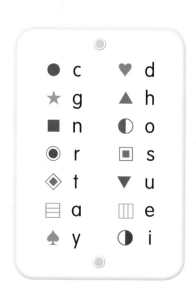

● c   ♥ d
★ g   ▲ h
■ n   ◑ o
◉ r   ▣ s
◈ t   ▼ u
▤ a   ▥ e
♠ y   ◑ i

e-learning

C. Match, ask, and answer.

A: How about having some hot dogs?
B: Sounds like a good idea.

1 hot dogs

waffles

popcorn

churros

ice cream

crackers

D. Work with your friends.

- Make a mini-book and talk with your friends while using it.

How about having some hot dogs?

Sounds like a good idea.

A Trip to New York

A. Listen and repeat the story.

B. Listen and number the pictures.

C. Read and correct the sentences.

1. Baba and Inky have waffles.

2. Baba and Inky go to a shopping mall.

3. The T-shirt is 7 dollars.

D. Choose an item and do a role-play.

☐　　　　☐　　　　☐

A. Listen and sing.

How Much Is This Coat?

I'm getting hungry.
  So am I. So am I.

How about having some hot dogs?
  Sounds like a good idea.

Look. Look. It's a flea market.
  Let's go and see.

How much is this coat?
  15, 15. It's 15 dollars.

B. Play a board game.

♥ How much is this _____?
- It's _____ dollars.

★ How about having some _____?
- Sounds like a good idea.

START

FINISH

Food Trucks

There are no waitresses, waiters, or tables, but you can enjoy delicious food. When you walk on the streets in America, you can find some trucks selling different kinds of food. People call them food trucks.

Why do people like to buy food from food trucks? Because it is fun to choose the food. The food is also easy to eat and cheap. What food trucks are you interested in?

Check It Out!

1. How are food trucks different from restaurants?
2. Why do people like to buy food from food trucks?

The Nearest Places

Let's Talk

A. Look, listen, and repeat.

It's getting dark. I'm tired.

Let's go to the hotel.

Where is the nearest bus stop?

It's over there.

Let's go to the hotel.

B. Listen and practice.

Where is the nearest bus stop?

1. bus stop
2. taxi stand
3. subway station
4. train station

C. Listen, point, and say.

A: Where is the nearest bus stop?
B: Look. It's over there.

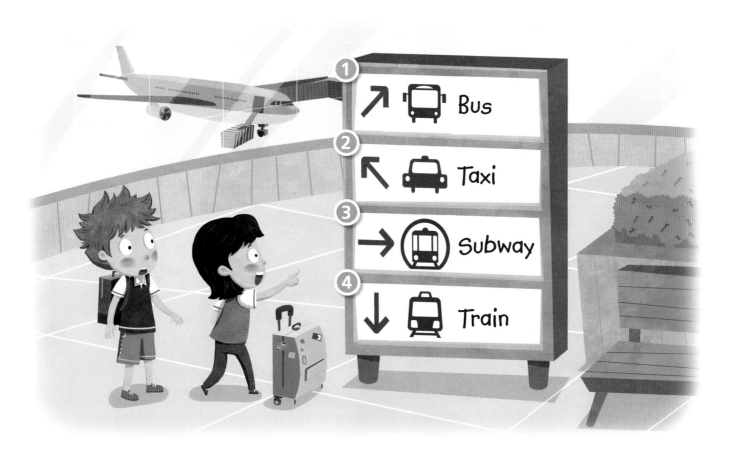

1. Bus
2. Taxi
3. Subway
4. Train

Let's Learn

A. Listen and chant.

Dark, dark. It's getting dark.

I'm tired.

Let's go to the hotel.

Where is the nearest bus stop?

It's over there. It's over there.

Where is the nearest subway station?

It's over there. It's over there.

B. Look and match.

Q: Where is the nearest _____ ?
A: It's over there.

① Platform 9

②

③

④

ⓐ bus stop

ⓑ taxi stand

ⓒ train station

ⓓ subway station

C. Roll the dice.
Then, ask and answer.

> A: Where is the nearest bus stop?
> B: It's over there.

① ⚀ bus stop

② ⚁ taxi stand

③ ⚂ subway station

④ ⚃ train station

⑤ ⚄ tram stop

⑥ ⚅ quay

D. Work with your friends.

- Guess what places your partner is looking for.

Plans for Tomorrow

Let's Talk

A. Look, listen, and repeat.

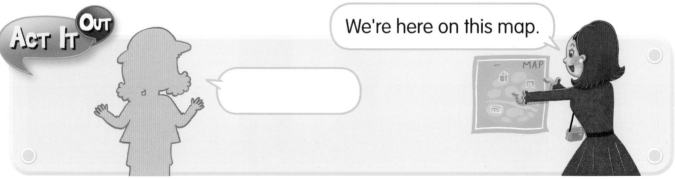

B. Listen and practice.

We're going to visit the palace.

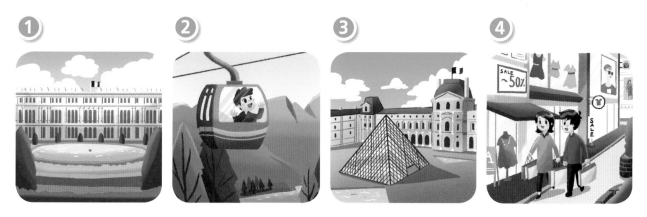

① visit the palace   ② take a cable car   ③ go to a museum   ④ go shopping

C. Listen, point, and say.

A: What are we going to do tomorrow?
B: We're going to visit the palace.

A. Listen and chant.

Where are we? Where are we?
  We're here.
  We're here on this map.

What are we going to do tomorrow?
  We're going to visit the palace.
What are we going to do tomorrow?
  We're going to take a cable car.

B. Listen and check True or False.

T: True   F: False

①

☐ T ☐ F

②

☐ T ☐ F

③

☐ T ☐ F

④

☐ T ☐ F

C. Match, ask, and answer.

A: What are we going to do tomorrow?
B: We're going to visit the palace.

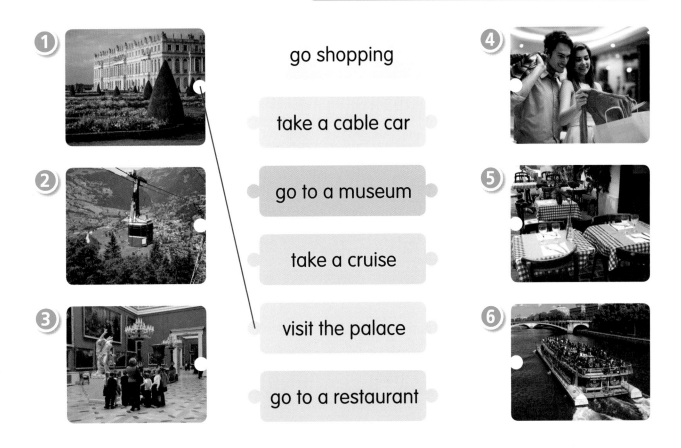

①

go shopping

take a cable car

②

go to a museum

take a cruise

③

visit the palace

go to a restaurant

④

⑤

⑥

D. Work with your friends.

- Talk about what you and your partner are going to do tomorrow.

To do:
1.
2.
3.

19 A Trip to Switzerland

A. Listen and repeat the story.

B. Listen and number the pictures.

C. Read and check.

1 What are Inky and Baba looking for?

a a tram stop　　　**b** a subway station　　　**c** a bus stop

2 What are Inky and Baba going to do tomorrow?

a take a cable car　　　**b** take a train　　　**c** take a cruise

D. Choose a type of transportation and do a role-play.

A. Listen and sing.

We're Going to Visit the Palace

It's getting dark. I'm tired.
  Let's go to the hotel.

Where are we?
  We're here on this map.

Where is the nearest bus stop?
  It's over there.

What are we going to do tomorrow?
  We're going to visit the palace.

B. Play a board game.

♥ Where is the nearest _____?
  - It's over there.

★ What are we going to do tomorrow?
  - We're going to _____.

A Traditional Swiss Food: Fondue

Have you ever eaten fondue, a traditional Swiss food? Fondue is a melted cheese dish. Long forks are used to eat it. Spear a bread cube and then dip it into the cheese and eat.

There is an interesting tradition. It says that if a woman drops her bread, she must kiss her neighbors. If a man does that, he must buy a bottle of wine. How about having some fondue with your family and friends?

Check It Out!

1. When eating fondue, what do people use?
2. If a man drops his bread into the cheese, what does he do according to tradition?

1. Listening

A. Listen and check.

①

a. ☐ b. ☐

②

a. ☐ b. ☐

③

a. ☐ b. ☐

④

a. ☐ b. ☐

⑤

a. ☐ b. ☐

⑥

a. ☐ b. ☐

B. Listen and answer the questions.

① What will the boy and girl eat?
   a. waffles   b. hot dogs   c. ice cream

② What are the boy and girl looking for?
   a. a subway station   b. a bus stop   c. a taxi stand

A. Look, listen, and reply.

①

②

③

④

B. Number the sentences in order and talk with your partner.

◯ It's 10 euros.

① Look. It's a flea market.

◯ How much is this sweater?

◯ Let's go and see.

A. Read and match.

1. How much is this coat? • • a. Not at all.

2. Do you mind if I send you an • • b. I like spring.
email?

3. Where is the nearest bus stop? • • c. Sounds like a good idea.

4. What season do you like the • • d. It's 20 euros.
most?

5. What are we going to do • • e. We're going to visit the
tomorrow? palace.

6. How about having some • • f. It's over there.
popcorn?

B. Read and check True or False.

Look. It's a flea market.

Let's go and see.

How much is this jacket?

It's 15 euros.

⋮

How about having some hot dogs?

Sounds like a good idea.

Amy   Harry

1. Amy and Harry are at a flea market. .... True ☐ False ☐

2. The price of the jacket is 15 euros. .... True ☐ False ☐

3. Amy suggests having some popcorn to Harry. .... True ☐ False ☐

hot dogs   fall   dress   call you
subway station   take a cable car

A. Write the words and phrases.

①

_____

②

_____

③

_____

④

_____

⑤

⑥

How much is this

_____

?

Where is
the nearest

_____

?

B. Write the answers.

① A: What season do you like the most?

B: _____

(winter / like / I / .)

② A: How about having some churros?

B: _____

(idea / a / like / sounds / good / .)

③ A: What are we going to do tomorrow?

B: _____

(going / to / we're / go / a / museum / to / .)

Syllabus

Lesson	Topic	Language	Key Vocabulary
Lesson 1	The Way to the Eiffel Tower	Excuse me. How can I get to the Eiffel Tower? - Go straight and turn right at the bookstore. Are we lost? - I'm not sure.	turn right at the bookstore turn right at the school turn left at the hospital turn left at the bank
Lesson 2	Where We Are From	Where are you from? - I'm from Canada. Would you like to join me? - Sure.	Canada Korea France China
Lesson 3	A Trip to London	Step Up 1 (Review Lessons 1-2) *Reading Time: An Icon of London: Double-Decker Red Buses	
Lesson 4	Travel Plans	How long will you stay? - We'll stay until next week. Are you traveling? - Yes, we are.	next week tomorrow this weekend next Friday
Lesson 5	Speaking a Foreign Language	Can you speak French? - No, I can't. [Yes, I can.] You speak English very well. - Thank you.	French Korean German English
Lesson 6	A Trip to Beijing	Step Up 2 (Review Lessons 4-5) *Reading Time: The Forbidden City	
Lesson 7	Famous Places	Is this a famous bakery? - Yes, it is. They look delicious, don't they? - Yes, they do.	bakery library hotel park
Lesson 8	The Juice You Want	What kind of juice do you want? - I want kiwi juice. Try this pie. - Thank you.	kiwi juice strawberry juice grape juice melon juice
Lesson 9	A Trip to Prague	Step Up 3 (Review Lessons 7-8) *Reading Time: Czech Marionettes	
Lesson 10	Assessment Test 1 (Review Lessons 1-9)		

Lesson	Topic	Language	Key Vocabulary
Lesson 11	The Four Seasons	What season do you like the most? - I like spring. What lovely weather! - Yes, it is.	spring summer fall winter
Lesson 12	Time to Say Goodbye	Do you mind if I take a picture with you? - Not at all. It was nice meeting you. - You, too. Good luck.	take a picture with you give you a hug send you an email call you
Lesson 13	A Trip to Brazil	Step Up 4 (Review Lessons 11-12) *Reading Time: The Rio Carnival in Brazil	
Lesson 14	The Price of the Dress	How much is this dress? - It's 20 euros. Look. It's a flea market. - Let's go and see.	dress T-shirt sweater coat
Lesson 15	Having Some Hot Dogs	How about having some hot dogs? - Sounds like a good idea. I'm getting hungry. - So am I.	hot dogs waffles churros popcorn
Lesson 16	A Trip to New York	Step Up 5 (Review Lessons 14-15) *Reading Time: Food Trucks	
Lesson 17	The Nearest Places	Where is the nearest bus stop? - It's over there. It's getting dark. I'm tired. - Let's go to the hotel.	bus stop taxi stand subway station train station
Lesson 18	Plans for Tomorrow	What are we going to do tomorrow? - We're going to visit the palace. Where are we? - We're here on this map.	visit the palace take a cable car go to a museum go shopping
Lesson 19	A Trip to Switzerland	Step Up 6 (Review Lessons 17-18) *Reading Time: A Traditional Swiss Food: Fondue	
Lesson 20	Assessment Test 2 (Review Lessons 11-19)		

Flashcard List

turn right at the bookstore	turn right at the school	turn left at the hospital
turn left at the bank	Canada	Korea
France	China	next week
tomorrow	this weekend	next Friday
French	Korean	German
English	bakery	library
hotel	park	kiwi juice
strawberry juice	grape juice	melon juice
spring	summer	fall
winter	take a picture with you	give you a hug
send you an email	call you	dress
T-shirt	sweater	coat
hot dogs	waffles	churros
popcorn	bus stop	taxi stand
subway station	train station	visit the palace
take a cable car	go to a museum	go shopping

Lesson 1 — The Way to the Eiffel Tower

	Vocabulary	Meaning	Sentence
1	turn right at the bookstore*	서점에서 우회전하다	Go straight and turn right at the bookstore.
2	turn right at the school*	학교에서 우회전하다	Go straight and turn right at the school.
3	turn left at the hospital*	병원에서 좌회전하다	Go straight and turn left at the hospital.
4	turn left at the bank*	은행에서 좌회전하다	Go straight and turn left at the bank.
5	turn right at the movie theater*	영화관에서 우회전하다	Go straight and turn right at the movie theater.
6	turn left at the restaurant*	식당에서 좌회전하다	Go straight and turn left at the restaurant.
7	we	우리는[가]	Are we lost?
8	lost	길을 잃은	Are we lost?
9	sure	확신하는	I'm not sure.
10	Excuse me.	실례합니다.	Excuse me.
11	get to	～에 도착하다	How can I get to the Eiffel Tower?
12	straight	똑바로	Go straight and turn right at the bookstore.

Lesson 2 — Where We Are From

	Vocabulary	Meaning	Sentence
1	Canada*	캐나다	I'm from Canada.
2	Korea*	대한민국	I'm from Korea.
3	France*	프랑스	I'm from France.
4	China*	중국	I'm from China.
5	Germany*	독일	I'm from Germany.
6	Japan*	일본	I'm from Japan.
7	Would you like ~ ?	～하시겠습니까?	Would you like to join me?
8	join	함께하다	Would you like to join me?
9	me	나를	Would you like to join me?
10	Sure.	그래요.	Sure.
11	where	어디에	Where are you from?
12	from	～에서	I'm from Canada.

Lesson 5 — Speaking a Foreign Language

	Vocabulary	Meaning	Sentence
1	French*	프랑스어	Can you speak French?
2	Korean*	한국어	Can you speak Korean?
3	German*	독일어	Can you speak German?
4	English*	영어	Can you speak English?
5	Chinese*	중국어	Can you speak Chinese?
6	Japanese*	일본어	Can you speak Japanese?
7	you	너, 당신	You speak English very well.
8	speak	말하다	You speak English very well.
9	very	매우	You speak English very well.
10	well	잘	You speak English very well.
11	Thank you.	감사합니다.	Thank you.
12	can't	～할 수 없다	No, I can't.

Lesson 6 — A Trip to Beijing

	Vocabulary	Meaning	Sentence
1	how long	(시간, 기간이) 얼마나	How long will you stay?
2	stay	머무르다	How long will you stay?
3	until	～까지	We'll stay until next Tuesday.
4	next Tuesday	다음 주 화요일	We'll stay until next Tuesday.
5	speak	말하다	You speak English very well.
6	can	～할 수 있다	Can you speak Chinese?
7	heart	중심부	It is located in the heart of Beijing, China.
8	large	큰	The Forbidden City is very large.
9	include	포함하다	It includes 90 palaces.
10	roof	지붕	The roofs of the buildings were made with yellow tiles.
11	tile	기와, 타일	The roofs of the buildings were made with yellow tiles.
12	emperor	황제	The reason is that yellow symbolized the emperor.

Lesson 3 — A Trip to London

	Vocabulary	Meaning	Sentence
1	lost	길을 잃은	Are we lost?
2	can	~할 수 있다	How can I get to Big Ben?
3	turn right at the restaurant	식당에서 우회전하다	Go straight and turn right at the restaurant.
4	join	함께하다	Would you like to join me?
5	where	어디에	Where are you from?
6	Korea	대한민국	I'm from Korea.
7	icon	상징, 아이콘	An Icon of London: Double-Decker Red Buses
8	story	층	They have two stories.
9	road	도로, 길	You can find a bus stop along all of the roads in London.
10	top	맨 위의	You are seated in the front row on the top deck of the bus.
11	sightseeing	관광	You can enjoy sightseeing in London much better.
12	ride	타다	Wouldn't it be fun to ride on a double-decker red bus?

Lesson 4 — Travel Plans

	Vocabulary	Meaning	Sentence
1	next week*	다음 주	We'll stay until next week.
2	tomorrow*	내일	We'll stay until tomorrow.
3	this weekend*	이번 주 주말	We'll stay until this weekend.
4	next Friday*	다음 주 금요일	We'll stay until next Friday.
5	this Wednesday*	이번 주 수요일	We'll stay until this Wednesday.
6	October 5*	10월 5일	We'll stay until October 5.
7	you	너희들	Are you traveling?
8	travel	여행하다	Are you traveling?
9	how long	(시간, 기간이) 얼마나	How long will you stay?
10	will	~할 것이다	How long will you stay?
11	stay	머무르다	We'll stay until next week.
12	until	~까지	We'll stay until next week.

Lesson 7 — Famous Places

	Vocabulary	Meaning	Sentence
1	bakery*	빵집	Is this a famous bakery?
2	library*	도서관	Is this a famous library?
3	hotel*	호텔	Is this a famous hotel?
4	park*	공원	Is this a famous park?
5	restaurant*	식당	Is this a famous restaurant?
6	museum*	박물관	Is this a famous museum?
7	they	그것들에[은]	They look delicious, don't they?
8	look	~해 보이다	They look delicious, don't they?
9	delicious	맛있는	They look delicious, don't they?
10	don't	~하지 않다	They look delicious, don't they?
11	this	이것이[은]	Is this a famous bakery?
12	famous	유명한	Is this a famous bakery?

Lesson 8 — The Juice You Want

	Vocabulary	Meaning	Sentence
1	kiwi juice*	키위주스	I want kiwi juice.
2	strawberry juice*	딸기주스	I want strawberry juice.
3	grape juice*	포도주스	I want grape juice.
4	melon juice*	멜론주스	I want melon juice.
5	apple juice*	사과주스	I want apple juice.
6	orange juice*	오렌지주스	I want orange juice.
7	try	해 보다, 먹어 보다	Try this pie.
8	this	(가까이 있는 것을 가리켜) 이	Try this pie.
9	pie	파이	Try this pie.
10	what	어떤	What kind of juice do you want?
11	kind	종류	What kind of juice do you want?
12	want	원하다	What kind of juice do you want?

Lesson 9   A Trip to Prague

	Vocabulary	Meaning	Sentence
1	famous	유명한	Is this a famous bakery?
2	bakery	빵집	Is this a famous bakery?
3	delicious	맛있는	They look delicious, don't they?
4	bread	빵	Try this bread.
5	juice	주스	What kind of juice do you want?
6	want	원하다	I want orange juice.
7	string	끈, 줄	It's a string puppet.
8	puppet	(인형극에 쓰이는) 인형	It's a string puppet.
9	move	움직이다	You can move its parts by using strings.
10	wizard	마법사	The marionettes represent wizards.
11	princess	공주	The marionettes represent princesses.
12	performance	공연	How about seeing a marionette performance?

Lesson 11   The Four Seasons

	Vocabulary	Meaning	Sentence
1	spring*	봄	I like spring.
2	summer*	여름	I like summer.
3	fall*	가을	I like fall.
4	winter*	겨울	I like winter.
5	what	(감탄문) 정말	What lovely weather!
6	lovely	아름다운	What lovely weather!
7	weather	날씨	What lovely weather!
8	what	(의문문) 어떤	What season do you like the most?
9	season	계절	What season do you like the most?
10	you	너, 당신	What season do you like the most?
11	like	좋아하다	What season do you like the most?
12	most	가장, 최고로	What season do you like the most?

Lesson 14   The Price of the Dress

	Vocabulary	Meaning	Sentence
1	dress*	드레스, 원피스	How much is this dress?
2	T-shirt*	티셔츠	How much is this T-shirt?
3	sweater*	스웨터	How much is this sweater?
4	coat*	코트	How much is this coat?
5	jacket*	재킷	How much is this jacket?
6	skirt*	치마	How much is this skirt?
7	look	보다	Look.
8	flea market	벼룩시장	It's a flea market.
9	let's	~하자	Let's go and see.
10	see	보다	Let's go and see.
11	how much	(양, 값이) 얼마	How much is this dress?
12	this	(가까이 있는 것을 가리켜) 이	How much is this dress?

Lesson 15   Having Some Hot Dogs

	Vocabulary	Meaning	Sentence
1	hot dog*	핫도그	How about having some hot dogs?
2	waffle*	와플	How about having some waffles?
3	churros*	추로스	How about having some churros?
4	popcorn*	팝콘	How about having some popcorn?
5	ice cream*	아이스크림	How about having some ice cream?
6	cracker*	크래커	How about having some crackers?
7	get	(어떤 상태가) 되다	I'm getting hungry.
8	hungry	배고픈	I'm getting hungry.
9	How about ~?	~는 어때요?	How about having some hot dogs?
10	some	조금	How about having some hot dogs?
11	sound like	~처럼 들리다	Sounds like a good idea.
12	idea	발상, 생각	Sounds like a good idea.

Lesson 12 — Time to Say Goodbye

	Vocabulary	Meaning	Sentence
1	take a picture with you*	너와 함께 사진을 찍다	Do you mind if I take a picture with you?
2	give you a hug*	너와 포옹하다	Do you mind if I give you a hug?
3	send you an email*	너에게 이메일을 보내다	Do you mind if I send you an email?
4	call you*	너에게 전화하다	Do you mind if I call you?
5	write a letter*	편지 쓰다	Do you mind if I write a letter?
6	send you a text message*	너에게 문자 메시지를 보내다	Do you mind if I send you a text message?
7	nice	좋은	It was nice meeting you.
8	meet	만나다	It was nice meeting you.
9	Good luck.	행운을 빌어.	Good luck.
10	mind	언짢아하다	Do you mind if I take a picture with you?
11	if	~면	Do you mind if I take a picture with you?
12	Not at all.	전혀 아니다.	Not at all.

Lesson 13 — A Trip to Brazil

	Vocabulary	Meaning	Sentence
1	what	(감탄문) 정말	What lovely weather!
2	lovely	아름다운	What lovely weather!
3	weather	날씨	What lovely weather!
4	what	(의문문) 어떤	What season do you like the most?
5	season	계절	What season do you like the most?
6	take a picture with you	너와 함께 사진을 찍다	Do you mind if I take a picture with you?
7	celebrate	축하하다	The carnival is held to celebrate the arrival of spring.
8	arrival	도착	The carnival is held to celebrate the arrival of spring.
9	parade	행진, 퍼레이드	The highlight of the carnival is the Samba Parade.
10	street	거리	The streets are filled with music and dancing.
11	attraction	명소	The carnival is one of the biggest attractions on the Earth.
12	Earth	지구	The carnival is one of the biggest attractions on the Earth.

Lesson 16 — A Trip to New York

	Vocabulary	Meaning	Sentence
1	How about ~?	~는 어때요?	How about having some hot dogs?
2	have	먹다	How about having some hot dogs?
3	sound like	~처럼 들리다	Sounds like a good idea.
4	flea market	벼룩시장	It's a flea market.
5	let's	~하자	Let's go and see.
6	how much	(양, 값이) 얼마	How much is this T-shirt?
7	waiter	웨이터	There are no waitresses, waiters, or tables.
8	truck	트럭	You can find some trucks selling different kinds of food.
9	call	~라고 부르다	People call them food trucks.
10	eat	먹다	The food is also easy to eat and cheap.
11	cheap	저렴한	The food is also easy to eat and cheap.
12	interested	관심 있는	What food trucks are you interested in?

Lesson 17 — The Nearest Places

	Vocabulary	Meaning	Sentence
1	bus stop*	버스 정류장	Where is the nearest bus stop?
2	taxi stand*	택시 정류장	Where is the nearest taxi stand?
3	subway station*	지하철역	Where is the nearest subway station?
4	train station*	기차역	Where is the nearest train station?
5	tram stop*	트램역	Where is the nearest tram stop?
6	quay*	부두, 선착장	Where is the nearest quay?
7	dark	어두운	It's getting dark.
8	tired	피곤한	I'm tired.
9	hotel	호텔	Let's go to the hotel.
10	where	어디에	Where is the nearest bus stop?
11	nearest	가장 가까운 (near의 최상급)	Where is the nearest bus stop?
12	over there	저쪽에	It's over there.

	Vocabulary	Meaning	Sentence
1	visit the palace*	궁을 방문하다	We're going to visit the palace.
2	take a cable car*	케이블카를 타다	We're going to take a cable car.
3	go to a museum*	박물관에 가다	We're going to go to a museum.
4	go shopping*	물건 사러 가다	We're going to go shopping.
5	go to a restaurant*	식당에 가다	We're going to go to a restaurant.
6	take a cruise*	유람선을 타다	We're going to take a cruise.
7	we	우리가[는]	Where are we?
8	here	여기에	We're here on this map.
9	on	~위에	We're here on this map.
10	map	지도	We're here on this map.
11	be going to	~을 할 것이다	What are we going to do tomorrow?
12	tomorrow	내일	What are we going to do tomorrow?

	Vocabulary	Meaning	Sentence
1	get	(어떤 상태가) 되다	It's getting dark.
2	tired	피곤한	I'm tired.
3	here	여기에	We're here on this map.
4	map	지도	We're here on this map.
5	nearest	가장 가까운 (near의 최상급)	Where is the nearest bus stop?
6	be going to	~을 할 것이다	What are we going to do tomorrow?
7	melted	녹은	Fondue is a melted cheese dish.
8	cheese	치즈	Fondue is a melted cheese dish.
9	spear	찌르다	Spear a bread cube.
10	cube	정육면체	Spear a bread cube.
11	dip	살짝 담그다	Dip it into the cheese.
12	bottle	병	He must buy a bottle of wine.

Memo

Memo

Answers

Student Book
Answers

Lesson 1 The Way to the Eiffel Tower
B. Look, read, and match.   p. 8

1. ⓒ   2. ⓑ   3. ⓐ

C. Fill in the blanks. Then, ask and answer.
                                                  p. 9

2. ⓔ   3. ⓕ   4. ⓐ   5. ⓑ   6. ⓒ

Lesson 2 Where We Are From
B. Listen and number the pictures.   p. 12

C. Match, ask, and answer.   p. 13

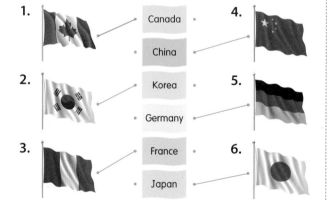

Lesson 3 A Trip to London
B. Listen and number the pictures.   p. 14

C. Read and circle.   p. 15

1. the restaurant   2. Korea

Reading Time   p. 17

1. It's the double-decker red bus.

2. It's a front-row seat on the top deck of the bus.

Lesson 4 Travel Plans
B. Listen and number.   p. 20

C. Match, ask, and answer.   p. 21

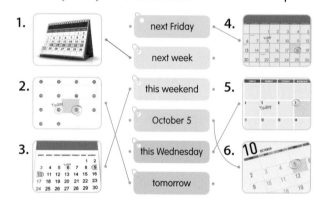

Lesson 5 Speaking a Foreign Language
B. Break the code and match.   p. 24

1. ⓒ   2. ⓑ   3. ⓓ   4. ⓐ

Lesson 6 A Trip to Beijing
B. Listen and number the pictures.   p. 26

C. Read and match.   p. 27

1. ⓐ   2. ⓑ

Reading Time   p. 29

1. It is located in the heart of Beijing, China.
2. The reason is that yellow symbolized the emperor.

Lesson 7 Famous Places

B. Look, read, and circle.   p. 32

1. bakery   2. library   3. hotel

C. Check, ask, and answer.   p. 33

2. library   3. hotel   4. park

5. restaurant   6. museum

Lesson 8 The Juice You Want

B. Listen and match.   p. 36

1. ⓑ   2. ⓒ   3. ⓐ

C. Go down the ladder. Then, ask and answer.   p. 37

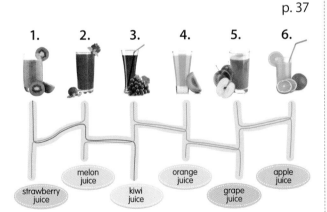

Lesson 9 A Trip to Prague

B. Listen and number the pictures.   p. 38

 ③   ①   ④   ②

C. Read and check True or False.   p. 39

1. True   2. False   3. True

Reading Time   p. 41

1. They are worked by strings.
2. They are made from wood or plaster.

Lesson 10 Assessment Test 1

Listening   p. 42

A. 1. b   2. a   3. a   4. b   5. a   6. b

B. 1. c   2. a

Speaking   p. 43

A. 1. I'm from France.
    2. We'll stay until tomorrow.
    3. Yes, it is.
    4. I want kiwi juice.

B. ② Go straight and turn left at the hospital.
    ③ Would you like to join me?
    ④ Sure.

Reading   p. 44

A. 1. b   2. f   3. d   4. e   5. a   6. c

B. 1. False   2. True   3. True

Writing   p. 45

A. 1. turn left at the bank
    2. China   3. next Friday
    4. strawberry juice
    5. Korean   6. library

B. 1. Go straight and turn right at the bookstore.
    2. I'm from Canada.
    3. I want kiwi juice.

Lesson 11 The Four Seasons

B. Look, read, and match.   p. 48

1. ⓑ   2. ⓒ   3. ⓓ   4. ⓐ

C. Go down the ladder. Then, ask and answer.

p. 49

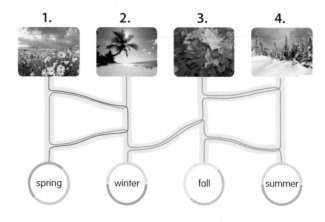

1.   2.   3.   4.

spring   winter   fall   summer

Lesson 12 Time to Say Goodbye
B. Listen and number the pictures.

p. 52

③ ④ ② ①

Lesson 13 A Trip to Brazil
B. Listen and number the pictures.

p. 54

① ③ ④ ②

C. Read and check.

p. 55

1. ⓑ   2. ⓒ

Reading Time

p. 57

1. It is to celebrate the arrival of spring.
2. It is the Samba Parade.

98

Lesson 14 The Price of the Dress
B. Listen and choose.

p. 60

1. ⓑ   2. ⓐ   3. ⓐ   4. ⓑ

Lesson 15 Having Some Hot Dogs
B. Break the code and read the sentences.

p. 64

1. hungry   2. hot dogs   3. churros
4. good idea

C. Match, ask, and answer.

p. 65

1.   2.   3.

hot dogs   waffles   popcorn   churros   ice cream   crackers

4.   5.   6.

Lesson 16 A Trip to New York
B. Listen and number the pictures.

p. 66

④ ③ ② ①

C. Read and correct the sentences.

p. 67

1. waffles → hot dogs
2. shopping mall → flea market
3. 7 → 5

Reading Time

p. 69

1. There are no waitresses, waiters, or tables, but you can enjoy delicious food.
2. It is fun to choose the food. It is also easy to eat and cheap.

Lesson 17 The Nearest Places

B. Look and match. p. 72

1. ⓒ   2. ⓐ   3. ⓑ   4. ⓓ

Lesson 18 Plans for Tomorrow

B. Listen and check True or False. p. 76

1. F   2. T   3. T   4. F

C. Match, ask, and answer. p. 77

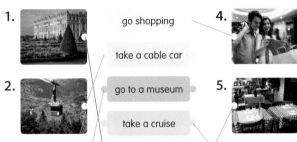

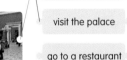

Lesson 19 A Trip to Switzerland

B. Listen and number the pictures. p. 78

①   ③   ④   ②

C. Read and check. p. 79

1. ⓒ   2. ⓐ

Reading Time p. 81

1. Long forks are used.
2. He buys a bottle of wine.

Lesson 20 Assessment Test 2

Listening p. 82

A. 1. b   2. a   3. a   4. b   5. b   6. a

B. 1. a   2. b

Speaking p. 83

A. 1. I like summer.   2. Not at all.

3. Sounds like a good idea.

4. We're going to go shopping.

B. ④ It's 10 euros.

③ How much is this sweater?

② Let's go and see.

Reading p. 84

A. 1. d   2. a   3. f   4. b   5. e   6. c

B. 1. True   2. True   3. False

Writing p. 85

A. 1. fall   2. call you

3. hot dogs   4. take a cable car

5. dress   6. subway station

B. 1. I like winter.

2. Sounds like a good idea.

3. We're going to go to a museum.

Workbook
Answers

Lesson 1 The Way to the Eiffel Tower

pp. 4~5

A. 1. turn right at the school
2. turn left at the hospital
3. turn left at the bank

B. 1. Are we lost?
2. turn right at the bookstore

C. 1. Are   2. sure
3. How   4. straight

D. 1. How   at the bookstore
2. How can   turn left at the bank
3. How can I get to
straight and turn left at the hospital

Lesson 2 Where We Are From

pp. 6~7

A. 1. Korea   2. Canada
3. China   4. France

B. 1. Would you like to join me?
2. Where are you from?

C. 1. join   2. Sure
3. Where   4. from

D. 1. from   Korea
2. are you from   from France
3. Where are you from?
I'm from China.

Lesson 3 A Trip to London

pp. 8~9

A. 1. lost   2. get to   turn right
3. join   4. Where   Korea

B. 1. I'm not sure.
2. Go straight and turn left at the bank.
3. Would you like to join me?
4. Where are you from?

Reading Time

1. story   2. ride
3. top   4. sightseeing
5. road   6. icon

Lesson 4 Travel Plans

pp. 10~11

A. 1. this weekend   2. next Friday
3. next week   4. tomorrow

B. 1. Are you traveling?
2. How long will you stay?

C. 1. traveling   2. we
3. long   4. until

D. 1. How long   this weekend
2. How long will   until next Friday
3. How long will you stay?
stay until tomorrow

Lesson 5 Speaking a Foreign Language

pp. 12~13

A. 1. Korean   2. German
3. English   4. French

B. 1. You speak English very well.
2. Can you speak French?

C. 1. well   2. Thank
3. speak   4. can't

D. 1. German   can't
2. speak English   I can't
3. Can you speak Korean?
I can't

Lesson 6 A Trip to Beijing

pp. 14~15

A. 1. stay   until
2. traveling   are
3. speak   4. Chinese

B. 1. We'll stay until this weekend.
2. Are you traveling?
3. You speak English very well.
4. Can you speak German?

Reading Time
1. ⓑ   2. ⓒ   3. ⓓ   4. ⓐ

Lesson 7 Famous Places

pp. 16~17

A. 1. hotel   2. park
3. library   4. bakery

B. 1. They look delicious, don't they?
2. Is this a famous bakery?

C. 1. delicious   2. do
3. bakery   4. Yes

D. 1. bakery   is
2. famous library   it is
3. Is this a famous hotel?
Yes, it is.

Lesson 8 The Juice You Want

pp. 18~19

A. 1. grape juice   2. kiwi juice
3. melon juice
4. strawberry juice

B. 1. Thank you.
2. What kind of juice do you want?

C. 1. pie   2. Thank
3. kind   4. want

D. 1. you want   kiwi juice
2. juice do you want
want strawberry juice
3. What kind of juice do you want?
I want grape juice.

Lesson 9 A Trip to Prague   pp. 20~21

A. 1. bakery   2. delicious   do
3. Try   4. juice   want

B. 1. Is this a famous library?
2. They look delicious, don't they?
3. Try this pie.
4. What kind of juice do you want?

Reading Time

1.   2.   3.   4.

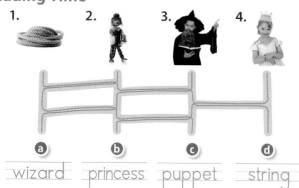

a. wizard   b. princess   c. puppet   d. string

Lesson 11 The Four Seasons   pp. 22~23

A. 1. winter   2. spring
3. fall   4. summer

B. 1. What lovely weather!
2. What season do you like the most?

C. 1. weather   2. it
3. season   4. spring

D. 1. What season   summer
2. What season do you like   like winter
3. What season do you like the most?
I like fall.

Lesson 12 Time to Say Goodbye   pp. 24~25

A. 1. send you an email
2. call you
3. give you a hug

B. 1. It was nice meeting you.
2. Not at all.

C. 1. meeting   2. too
3. mind   4. all

D. 1. send you an email   Not
2. if I give you a hug   Not at
3. you mind if I call you   Not at all.

Lesson 13 A Trip to Brazil   pp. 26~27

A. 1. weather   2. most   summer
3. mind   Not   4. was

B. 1. What lovely weather!
2. What season do you like the most?
3. Do you mind if I send you an email?
4. It was nice meeting you.

Reading Time

l	o	t	a	c	e	b	i	k
d	c	g	j	e	v	t	s	N
m	A	s	b	l	r	y	t	o
U	n	y	h	e	L	o	r	e
r	i	p	a	b	n	g	e	w
o	v	p	a	r	a	d	e	q
g	l	e	d	a	c	i	t	i
z	E	a	r	t	h	f	j	r
p	r	a	c	e	l	n	o	B

Lesson 14 The Price of the Dress   pp. 28~29

A. 1. coat   2. sweater

3. dress   4. T-shirt

B. 1. Let's go and see.

2. How much is this dress?

C. 1. flea market   2. Let's

3. much   4. euros

D. 1. this T-shirt   euros

2. is this coat   20 euros

3. How much is this dress?

It's 15 euros.

Lesson 15 Having Some Hot Dogs

pp. 30~31

A. 1. waffles   2. churros

3. popcorn   4. hot dogs

B. 1. I'm getting hungry.

2. How about having some hot dogs?

C. 1. hungry   2. am

3. hot dogs   4. idea

D. 1. some waffles   good idea

2. having some popcorn

a good idea

3. How about having some churros?

Sounds like a good idea?

Lesson 16 A Trip to New York   pp. 32~33

A. 1. hungry   So

2. hot dogs   Sounds

3. Let's   4. How much

B. 1. I'm getting hungry.

2. How about having some waffles?

3. It's a flea market.

4. How much is this dress?

Reading Time

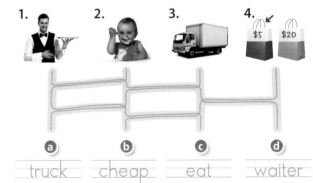

@a truck   @b cheap   @c eat   @d waiter

Lesson 17 The Nearest Places   pp. 34~35

A. 1. train station   2. taxi stand

3. bus stop   4. subway station

B. 1. Let's go to the hotel.

2. It's over there.

C. 1. dark   2. Let's

3. nearest   4. over

D. 1. train station   there

2. the nearest subway station

over there

3. Where is the nearest taxi stand?
   It's over there.

Lesson 18 Plans for Tomorrow   pp. 36~37

A. 1. go to a museum
   2. go shopping
   3. visit the palace
   4. take a cable car

B. 1. Where are we?
   2. What are we going to do tomorrow?

C. 1. Where   2. here
   3. going   4. visit

D. 1. going to do   go shopping
   2. we going to do tomorrow
      going to go to a museum
   3. What are we going to do tomorrow?
      We're going to take a cable car.

Lesson 19 A Trip to Switzerland   pp. 38~39

A. 1. tired   2. on
   3. nearest   over
   4. What   going

B. 1. Let's go to the hotel.
   2. We're here on this map.
   3. Where is the nearest subway station?
   4. We're going to visit the palace.

Reading Time

1. spear   2. bottle
3. cube   4. dip
5. melted   6. cheese

Final Test
English Town Book 2

1. ②	2. ⑤	3. ⑤	4. ①	5. ⑤
6. ②	7. ④	8. ①	9. ③	10. ④
11. ④	12. ②	13. ④	14. ④	15. ①
16. ④	17. ④	18. ③		
19. long		20. much		

Final Test_English Town Book 2

Part 3 - Reading

[13-14] Look and choose the right one for the blank.

13

A: Where are you from?
B: I'm from _____.

① Canada   ② China   ③ France
④ Korea   ⑤ Germany

14

A: What kind of juice do you want?
B: _____

① Yes, I do.
② You want kiwi juice.
③ I don't like strawberry.
④ I want strawberry juice.
⑤ I want orange juice.

[15-16] Read and answer the questions.

Ming: You speak English very well.
Suho: Thank you.
Ming: _____ you speak Chinese?
Suho: No, I can't.

15 What is the right word for the blank?

① Can   ② Do   ③ Are
④ Is   ⑤ Would

16 What language can Suho speak?

① Korean   ② French   ③ Chinese
④ English   ⑤ German

[17-18] Read and answer the questions.

Tom: It's getting dark. I'm tired.
Sarah: Let's go to the hotel.
Tom: Where is the nearest bus stop?
Sarah: It's _____ there.

17 What does Sarah suggest to Tom?

① Taking a taxi
② Going to the bus stop
③ Getting some rest
④ Going to the hotel
⑤ Having some food

18 What is the right word for the blank?

① on   ② in   ③ over
④ under   ⑤ beside

Part 4 - Writing

[19-20] Choose and write the right word.

much   nice   long   kind

19 A: How _____ will you stay?
B: We'll stay until this weekend.

20 A: How _____ is this skirt?
B: It's 5 euros.

Final Test
English Town Book 2

Class	Name	Score
		/20

[1-2] Look, listen, and choose the right one.

1   ① ② ③ ④ ⑤

2    ① ② ③ ④ ⑤

[3-4] Listen and choose the right picture.

3 ①   ②   ③
④   ⑤

4 ①   ②   ③
④   ⑤

[5-6] Look, listen, and choose the right conversation.

5   ① ② ③ ④ ⑤

6   ① ② ③ ④ ⑤

[7-8] Listen and find the correct answer to the question.

7   Where are they?

① At the library
② At the park
③ At the museum
④ At the bakery
⑤ At the hospital

8   What are they doing?

① They are taking a picture.
② They are sending an email.
③ They are calling someone.
④ They are sending a text message.
⑤ They are writing a letter.

[9-10] Listen and choose the wrong conversation.

9 ① ② ③ ④ ⑤

10 ① ② ③ ④ ⑤

[11-12] Listen and choose the best response to the last sentence.

11 ① We're going to visit the palace.
② We're here on this map.
③ I'm from Canada.
④ We'll stay until next week.
⑤ Yes, we are.

12 ① I want kiwi juice.   ② I like spring.
③ Not at all.   ④ Yes, it is.
⑤ It's over there.

ENGLISH TOWN

FOR EVERYONE

BOOK

2

WORKBOOK

YBM

ENGLiSH TOWN

FOR EVERYONE

BOOK

2

WORKBOOK

Contents

The Way to the Eiffel Tower

Let's Write

A. Write the phrases.

①

②

③

turn right at the school   turn left at the hospital
turn left at the bank

B. Choose and write.

*R: Rachel   RM: Rachel's mom   M: Mathis

1. R : _____

   RM: I'm not sure.

2. RM: Excuse me. How can I get to the Eiffel Tower?

   M: Go straight and _____
   _____.

- Are we lost?
- turn right at the bookstore

4

C. Complete the sentences.

sure   are   straight   how

1. _____ we lost?

2. I'm not _____ .

3. _____ can I get to the Eiffel Tower?

4. Go _____ and turn right at the bookstore.

D. Look and write.

Example   1   2   3

Example

A: How can I get to the Eiffel Tower?

B: Go straight and turn right at the school .

1. A: _____ can I get to the Eiffel Tower?

   B: Go straight and turn right _____ .

2. A: _____ I get to the Eiffel Tower?

   B: Go straight and _____ .

3. A: _____ the Eiffel Tower?

   B: Go _____ .

Where We Are From

Let's Write

A. Write the words.

①

②

③

④

_____   _____   _____   _____

Canada   Korea   France   China

B. Choose and write.

*M: Mathis   R: Rachel

1. M: _____
   _____
   _____

   R : Sure.

2. M: _____

   R : I'm from Canada.

• Where are you from?
• Would you like to join me?

C. Complete the sentences.

1 Would you like to _____ me?

2 _____ .

3 _____ are you from?

4 I'm _____ Canada.

D. Look and write.

Example   **1**    **2**    **3**

Example

A: Where are you ___from___ ?

B: I'm from ___Canada___ .

1. A: Where are you _____?

   B: I'm from _____ .

2. A: Where _____ ?

   B: I'm _____ .

3. A: _____

   B: _____

A Trip to London

Let's Write

A. Write the words and number the pictures.

① Baba: Are we _____ ?

Inky: I'm not sure.

② Inky: Excuse me. How can I _____ Big Ben?

Mr. Gee: Go straight and _____ at the restaurant.

③ Inky: Would you like to _____ me?

Mr. Gee: Sure.

④ Mr. Gee: _____ are you from?

Baba: I'm from _____ .

turn right

get to

lost

Korea

where

join

8

B. Unscramble the words and complete the dialogs.

1 A: Are we lost?

B: _____

(not / sure / I'm / .)

2 A: Excuse me. How can I get to Big Ben?

B: _____

(at / and / go / left / the / straight / turn / bank / .)

3 A: _____

(you / like / join / to / would / me / ?)

B: Sure.

4 A: _____

(you / are / from / where / ?)

B: I'm from France.

Reading Time

- **Write the words.**

1. _____

2. _____

3. _____

4. _____

5. _____

6. _____

sightseeing

icon

ride

road

story

top

Travel Plans

Let's Write

A. Write the words and phrases.

next week   this weekend   tomorrow   next Friday

B. Choose and write.

*M: Mathis   R: Rachel

1. M: _____

   R : Yes, we are.

2. M: _____
   _____

   R : We'll stay until next week.

- Are you traveling?
- How long will you stay?

C. Complete the sentences.

until   we   long   traveling

① Are you _____ ?

② Yes, _____ are.

③ How _____ will you stay?

④ We'll stay _____ next week.

D. Look and write.

Example

1

2

3

Example

A: How long will you stay?

B: We'll stay until next week .

1. A: _____ will you stay?

   B: We'll stay until _____ .

2. A: _____ you stay?

   B: We'll stay _____ .

3. A: _____

   B: We'll _____ .

Lesson 5 · Speaking a Foreign Language

Let's Write

A. Write the words.

①

②

③

④

English   Korean   German   French

B. Choose and write.

*R: Rachel   M: Mathis

1. R : _____

   M : Thank you.

2. M : _____

   R : No, I can't.

- Can you speak French?
- You speak English very well.

C. Complete the sentences.

speak   can't   well   thank

1 You speak English very _____ .

2 _____ you.

3 Can you _____ French?

4 No, I _____ .

D. Look and write.

Example   **1**   **2**   **3**

Example

A: Can you speak __French__ ?

B: No, I __can't__ .

1. A: Can you speak _____ ?

   B: No, I _____ .

2. A: Can you _____ ?

   B: No, _____ .

3. A: _____

   B: No, _____ .

A Trip to Beijing

Let's Write

A. **Write the words and number the pictures.**

1 Mr. Pan: How long will you _____?

Baba: We'll stay _____ next Tuesday.

2 Mr. Pan: Are you _____?

Baba: Yes, we _____.

3 Inky: You _____ English very well.

Mr. Pan: Thank you.

4 Mr. Pan: Can you speak _____?

Inky: No, I can't.

are

traveling

stay

Chinese

speak

until

B. **Unscramble the words and complete the dialogs.**

1 A: How long will you stay?

B: _____

(stay / weekend / we'll / this / until / .)

2 A: _____

(traveling / are / you / ?)

B: Yes, we are.

3 A: _____

(very / you / English / well / speak / .)

B: Thank you.

4 A: _____

(German / can / speak / you / ?)

B: No, I can't.

Reading Time

• **Match the pictures with the words.**

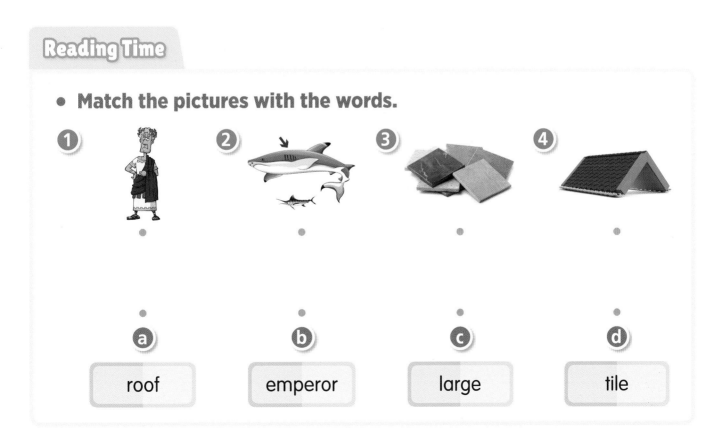

1   **2**   **3**   **4**

a   **b**   **c**   **d**

roof   emperor   large   tile

Lesson 7 Famous Places

Let's Write

A. Write the words.

①

②

③

④

park   bakery   hotel   library

B. Choose and write.

*R: Rachel   RM: Rachel's mom   M: Mathis

1. R : _____

   RM: Yes, they do.

2. RM: _____

   M: Yes, it is.

- Is this a famous bakery?
- They look delicious, don't they?

16

C. Complete the sentences.

bakery	delicious	yes	do

1 They look _____, don't they?

2 Yes, they _____.

3 Is this a famous _____?

4 _____, it is.

D. Look and write.

Example

1

2

3

Example

A: Is this a famous ___park___?

B: Yes, it ___is___.

1. A: Is this a famous _____?

   B: Yes, it _____.

2. A: Is this a _____?

   B: Yes, _____.

3. A: _____

   B: _____

Lesson 8

The Juice You Want

Let's Write

A. Write the words.

1

2

3

4

_____

_____

_____

_____

> melon juice   strawberry juice   grape juice   kiwi juice

B. Choose and write.

*L: Leo   R: Rachel   RM: Rachel's mom

1. L : Try this pie.

   R : _____

2. RM: _____

   _____

   R : I want kiwi juice.

   - Thank you.
   - What kind of juice do you want?

18

C. Complete the sentences.

1 Try this _____ .

2 _____ you.

3 What _____ of juice do you want?

4 I _____ kiwi juice.

D. Look and write.

Example   **1**   **2**   **3**

Example

A: What kind of juice do __you want__ ?

B: I want __melon juice__ .

1. A: What kind of juice do _____ ?

   B: I want _____ .

2. A: What kind of _____ ?

   B: I _____ .

3. A: _____

   B: _____

A Trip to Prague

Let's Write

A. Write the words and number the pictures.

1 Baba: Is this a famous _____ ?

Mr. Goat: Yes, it is.

2 Inky: They look _____ , don't they?

Baba: Yes, they _____ .

3 Mr. Bear: _____ this bread.

Baba: Thank you.

4 Baba: What kind of _____ do you want?

Inky: I _____ orange juice.

delicious

try

bakery

want

juice

do

B. Unscramble the words and complete the dialogs.

1 A: _____
(is / a / library / famous / this / ?)
B: Yes, it is.

2 A: _____
(look / don't / they / they / delicious / , / ?)
B: Yes, they do.

3 A: _____
(this / try / pie / .)
B: Thank you.

4 A: _____
(juice / what / want / you / kind / of / do / ?)
B: I want grape juice.

Reading Time

- **Do ghost leg and write the words.**

princess

string

puppet

wizard

Lesson 11 The Four Seasons

Let's Write

A. Write the words.

①

②

③

④

summer winter spring fall

B. Choose and write.

*R: Rachel   RM: Rachel's mom   M: Mathis

1. R : _____

   RM: Yes, it is.

2. M: _____

   R : I like spring.

- What season do you like the most?
- What lovely weather!

C. Complete the sentences.

spring season weather it

1 What lovely _____ !

2 Yes, _____ is.

3 What _____ do you like the most?

4 I like _____ .

D. Look and write.

Example

1

2

3

Example

A: What season do you like the most?

B: I like spring .

1. A: _____ do you like the most?

   B: I like _____ .

2. A: _____ the most?

   B: I _____ .

3. A: _____

   B: _____

Time to Say Goodbye

Let's Write

A. Write the phrases.

_____

_____

call you   send you an email   give you a hug

B. Choose and write.

Rachel & Mathis

* RM: Rachel's mom   M: Mathis   R: Rachel

1. RM: _____

_____

M: You, too. Good luck.

2. R : Do you mind if I take a picture with you?

_____

M: _____

- It was nice meeting you.
- Not at all.

C. Complete the sentences.

too   all   mind   meeting

1. It was nice _____ you.

2. You, _____ . Good luck.

3. Do you _____ if I take a picture with you?

4. Not at _____ .

D. Look and write.

Example   1   2   3

Example

A: Do you mind if I take a picture with you ?

B: Not at all.

1. A: Do you mind if I _____ ?

   B: _____ at all.

2. A: Do you mind _____ ?

   B: _____ all.

3. A: Do _____ ?

   B: _____

A Trip to Brazil

Let's Write

A. Write the words and number the pictures.

① Baba: What lovely _____ !

Inky: Yes, it is.

② Inky: What season do you like the _____ ?

Baba: I like _____ .

③ Inky: Do you _____ if I take a picture with you?

Tucan: _____ at all.

④ Inky: It _____ nice meeting you.

Tucan: You, too.

not

summer

mind

was

most

weather

B. Unscramble the words and complete the dialogs.

1 A: _____

(lovely / what / weather / !)

B: Yes, it is.

2 A: _____

(do / like / season / most / the / what / you / ?)

B: I like winter.

3 A: _____

(if / you / send / email / do / an / mind / I / you / ?)

B: Not at all.

4 A: _____

(meeting / you / was / nice / it / .)

B: You, too. Good luck.

Reading Time

- **Find out the words.**

c_____

E_____

l	o	t	a	c	e	b	i	k
d	c	g	j	e	v	t	s	N
m	A	s	b	l	r	y	t	o
U	n	y	h	e	L	o	r	e
r	i	p	a	b	n	g	e	w
o	v	p	a	r	a	d	e	q
g	l	e	d	a	c	i	t	i
z	E	a	r	t	h	f	j	r
p	r	a	c	e	l	n	o	B

p_____

s_____

The Price of the Dress

Let's Write

A. Write the words.

①

②

③

④

sweater   coat   T-shirt   dress

B. Choose and write.

*R: Rachel   RM: Rachel's mom   C: Corinne

1. R : Look. It's a flea market.

    RM: _____

2. RM: _____

    C : It's 20 euros.

    • How much is this dress?
    • Let's go and see.

C. Complete the sentences.

let's flea market euros much

1 Look. It's a _____ .

2 _____ go and see.

3 How _____ is this dress?

4 It's 20 _____ .

D. Look and write.

Example

€10

1 €5

2 €20

3 €15

Example

A: How much is _this sweater_ ?

B: It's 10 _euros_ .

1. A: How much is _____ ?

   B: It's 5 _____ .

2. A: How much _____ ?

   B: It's _____ .

3. A: _____

   B: _____

Having Some Hot Dogs

Let's Write

A. Write the words.

①

②

③

④

hot dogs   waffles   churros   popcorn

B. Choose and write.

* R: Rachel   RM: Rachel's mom

1. R : _____

    RM: So am I.

2. RM: _____

    R : Sounds like a good idea.

- How about having some hot dogs?
- I'm getting hungry.

C. Complete the sentences.

idea   hungry   am   hot dogs

① I'm getting _____ .

② So _____ I.

③ How about having some _____ ?

④ Sounds like a good _____ .

D. Look and write.

Example

①

②

③

Example

A: How about having   some hot dogs   ?

B: Sounds like a   good idea   .

1. A: How about having _____ ?

   B: Sounds like a _____ .

2. A: How about _____ ?

   B: Sounds like _____ .

3. A: _____

   B: _____

Let's Write

A. Write the words and number the pictures.

1. Baba: I'm getting _____ .

   Inky: _____ am I.

2. Inky: How about having some _____?

   Baba: _____ like a good idea.

3. Baba: Look. It's a flea market.

   Inky: _____ go and see.

4. Baba: _____ is this T-shirt?

   Ms. Mu: It's 5 dollars.

hungry

let's

sounds

hot dogs

so

how much

B. **Unscramble the words and complete the dialogs.**

1 A: _____
(I'm / hungry / getting / .)
B: So am I.

2 A: _____
(some / how / having / waffles / about / ?)
B: Sounds like a good idea.

3 A: Look. _____
(it's / flea market / a / .)
B: Let's go and see.

4 A: _____
(is / how / this / much / dress / ?)
B: It's 10 dollars.

Reading Time

• **Do ghost leg and write the words.**

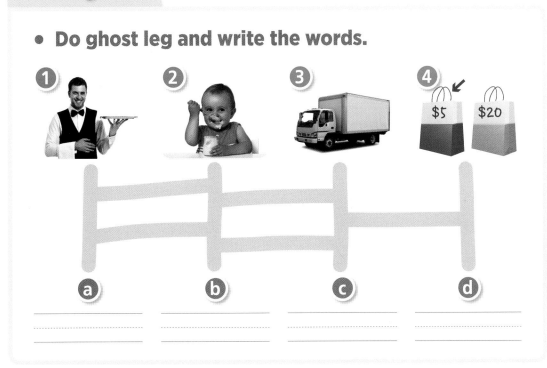

waiter

eat

cheap

truck

a _____ b _____ c _____ d _____

The Nearest Places

Let's Write

A. Write the words.

 ①

 ②

 ③

 ④

_____

_____

_____

_____

| subway station | bus stop | train station | taxi stand |

B. Choose and write.

* R: Rachel   RM: Rachel's mom   J: Jean

1. R : It's getting dark. I'm tired.

   RM: _____

2. RM: Where is the nearest bus stop?

   J : _____

- Let's go to the hotel.
- It's over there.

34

C. Complete the sentences.

nearest   over   dark   let's

1 It's getting _____ .

2 _____ go to the hotel.

3 Where is the _____ bus stop?

4 It's _____ there.

D. Look and write.

Example   **1**   **2**   **3**

Example

A: Where is the nearest ___bus stop___ ?

B: It's over ___there___ .

1. A: Where is the nearest _____ ?

   B: It's over _____ .

2. A: Where is _____ ?

   B: It's _____ .

3. A: _____

   B: _____

18 Plans for Tomorrow

Let's Write

A. Write the phrases.

①

②

③

④

_____
_____

visit the palace   go shopping
take a cable car   go to a museum

B. Choose and write.

*R: Rachel   RM: Rachel's mom

1. R : _____
RM: We're here on this map.

2. R : _____

RM: We're going to visit the palace.

- What are we going to do tomorrow?
- Where are we?

C. Complete the sentences.

1 _____ are we?

2 We're _____ on this map.

3 What are we _____ to do tomorrow?

4 We're going to _____ the palace.

D. Look and write.

Example   **1**   **2**   **3**

Example

A: What are we ___going to do___ tomorrow?

B: We're going to ___visit the palace___ .

1. A: What are we _____ tomorrow?

   B: We're going to _____ .

2. A: What are _____ ?

   B: We're _____ .

3. A: _____

   B: _____

A Trip to Switzerland

Let's Write

A. Write the words and number the pictures.

1. Baba: It's getting dark. I'm _____ .

   Inky: Let's go to the hotel.

2. Baba: Where are we?

   Inky: We're here _____ this map.

3. Inky: Where is the _____ bus stop?

   Mr. Munk: It's _____ there.

4. Baba: _____ are we going to do tomorrow?

   Inky: We're _____ to take a cable car.

on

going

over

what

tired

nearest

B. Unscramble the words and complete the dialogs.

1 A: It's getting dark. I'm tired.

B: _____

(the / go / hotel / to / let's / .)

2 A: Where are we?

B: _____

(map / this / on / we're / here / .)

3 A: _____

(is / subway station / the / where / nearest / ?)

B: It's over there.

4 A: What are we going to do tomorrow?

B: _____

(to / visit / going / the / we're / palace / .)

Reading Time

- **Write the words.**

1. _____

2. _____

3. _____

4. _____

5. _____

6. _____

melted

cheese

spear

cube

dip

bottle

Memo

ENGLISH TOWN

BOOK 2

ENGLISH TOWN BOOK 2

English Town is a spoken English course comprised of a series of 9 books, specifically designed for elementary school students.

- Learning English in a communicative way and in an easy manner
- Focused approach to new words, expressions, and dialogs
- Fun to sing and chant together
- Simple but effective games and activities
- Exciting stories

Components

· Student Book
· Workbook
· Final Test
· Teacher's Guide including teaching resources
· Online (www.ybmenglishtown.com)
  Interactive e-book for teachers and students
  E-learning for self-study

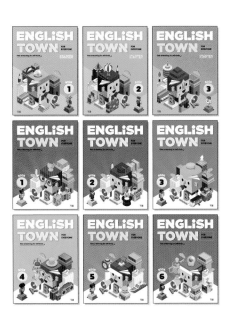

www.ybmenglishtown.com

YBM